T0159423

HOW TO TRAIN YOUR BOSS TO ROLL OVER

Tips for Becoming Top Dog

Wendy Diamond

Entrepreneur and Founder of Animal Fair Media, Inc.

CHANGING LIVES PRESS

CHANGING LIVES PRESS
50 Public Square #1600
Cleveland, OH 44113
www.changinglivespress.com

Library of Congress Cataloging-in-Publication Data is available
through the Library of Congress.

ISBN: 978-0-9882476-7-3

Copyright © 2013 by Wendy Diamond

Editor: Lisa Espinoza

Cover and Interior design: Gary A. Rosenberg
www.thebookcouple.com

Printed in the United States of America

10   9   8   7   6   5   4   3   2   1

CONTENTS

I would like to dedicate this book to every inspiring person and animal I've had the fortune of encountering throughout my life. Good souls come in all shapes and sizes—with two legs and four legs. I am truly grateful for the ups and downs. No matter how many times I've had to roll over or jump through hoops, it has helped me appreciate my experience to the fullest.

This book is also dedicated to my loving pets that inspire me each day in this "dog eat dog" business world—Pasha, Baby Hope, and Lucky (now in doggie heaven). Their daily unconditional love gives me the continual energy to work and fight for a world where there are no homeless and disenfranchised animals. This book also honors my mom and beloved dad—they are the reason I'm here and have made me the person I've become.

Fortunately, my career does not put me in a dangerous line of fire, and this is why I would like to also dedicate this book to all the brave veterans who have worked and fought so selflessly. Many have returned with PTSD after defending democracy and freedom. A bark out to all the amazing service and therapy dogs that bring peace and protection to our veterans, just as these heroic soldiers have done for us!

Dog Bless

"If there are no dogs in Heaven,
then when I die I want to
go where they went."

—WILL ROGERS

INTRODUCTION

W E ARE ANIMALS. ANIMALS BY NATURE and animals in business. Whoever coined the timeless phrase "dog-eat-dog world" perhaps offered the greatest piece of business advice anyone could ever hear. No matter how humans approach any situation, their animal instincts kick in. Let's expand upon the dog-eat-dog with a touch of civility . . . human civility that is. Less eating and more getting ahead.

During my twelve years as President and Founder of *Animal Fair* media, I have experienced firsthand this dog-eat-dog society we are living in while earning and coining the professional title "Chief Pet Officer" (CPO). Everyone wants a "C" in front of his or her title—think of a canine. But little did I know *then* that becoming an Alpha Dog in my career would teach me more professional lessons than I ever could have imagined learning, even in our country's top business schools. Forget Harvard Business School—I'm a graduate with honors from the School of Hard Knocks. In the business world, as in the animal world, competition

1

for the top spot is fierce. You get extra credit if you're a "b*tch"—yes, that means female Alpha Dog—because everywhere you look, there is another ambitious Alpha Dog (or Alpha B*tch) barking their way to the top, attempting to claim more profitable business territory.

Native Americans have a chief, football players have a coach, orchestras have a conductor, and conglomerates have a CEO or president. No matter what you call them, they're Alpha Dogs. An Alpha Dog is always leader of the pack. Alpha Dogs dominate, but that doesn't necessarily mean they have to be aggressive or large in stature —Napoleon anyone? Whatever the size, the Alpha Dog is where the proverbial buck stops. You want them to notice you and like your work. You want them to give you the perks and promotions you deserve. So how can you gain their respect and train that Alpha Dog in the workplace to do your bidding? You don't need Cesar Millan—his domain is real dogs. You need me, Wendy Diamond, whose domain is over a decade of experience working with animals, both the two-legged and the four-legged varieties.

How to Train Your Boss to Roll Over is an entertaining and practical little guidebook for employees who want to get ahead in the work world—and let's be honest, who doesn't want that? Whether you work for a "mom and pop" company, a Fortune 500 corporation, or are an entrepreneur trying to land that big client, *How to Train Your Boss to Roll Over* provides humorous training tips that will help you get the Top Dog in your company, or that hesitant potential client, to roll over. This handbook is the perfect gift for employees, friends, or family members who are in the process of landing, or have just landed, a new job opportunity or promotion. By taking a fresh look at the business world through the lens of the canine kingdom, you will learn how to woo and win over your Alpha Dog and gain the success you desire in the workplace.

How do you get yourself adopted if you're still in the pound? Once adopted, how can you get your Alpha Dog to think of you for that promotion or fill that empty corner office you've been eyeing? How do you politely tell your employer "no" if he or she insists on piling on work that's outside your job description or constantly asks you to stay late on Friday nights? *How to Train Your Boss to Roll Over* answers these questions and more while giving you a professional edge. It's time to put on your trainer's hat and get to work.

The training tips and advice in *How to Train Your Boss to Roll Over* will help you do just that. But remember—some dogs do bite! So enjoy training your Alpha Dog, but do so at your own risk!

"Happiness is a warm puppy."
—CHARLES M. SCHULZ

BEFORE A COMPANY ADOPTS YOU AS AN EMPLOYEE

S O YOU'RE STILL IN THE POUND with all the other unadopted dogs looking for a work home. If you've been there long enough, you know it can be discouraging to watch other dogs get adopted and leave the pound. Your turn will come. Don't be content to hang around and snooze; it's important to keep cruising for crumbs. Scavengers never give up. They also never go hungry. Get yourself out there where you can be seen by potential employers. And check out these hints that will help nudge just the right company into adopting you. Why shouldn't they? You're talented and creative. One look into your adorable puppy dog eyes and they'll know you're the right fit for their company. And then you're just one step closer to training your Alpha Dog, and maybe even becoming the Alpha Dog you've always wanted to be.

Forget the Past—Think Like a Dog

Dogs have outstanding scent memory and can even

remember specific sounds and voices for decades, but rarely do dogs dwell in the past—that's a human condition. If you're going to land that next big job or start your company or business, you cannot dwell in the past. If you were laid off, fired, or quit, it's time to move forward. Picture a dog that has been tossed from shelter to shelter—a greyhound who was once forced to race or a pit bull that was made to fight. These dogs have to forget those ugly memories and live in the present, not the past. The same goes for you if you want to be ready to return to the dog-eat-dog working world.

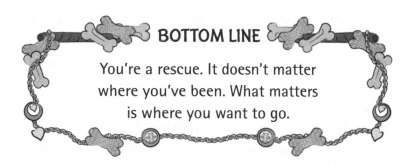

BOTTOM LINE

You're a rescue. It doesn't matter where you've been. What matters is where you want to go.

The Doggone Truth About Interviews, Resumes & Rufferences

When applying for a position within a company or hunting down a client, it's your responsibility to do the digging and research your company of interest. No one is going to throw you a bone, so be prepared. And now that we have Bing and Google, there are no excuses *not* to be prepared. Educate yourself on what position you're vying for. By finding out more about the "breed" of employer executing your final employment decision, you will gain an edge on the competition and impress the powers that be. Is she a friendly golden retriever type who wants to talk sports and hobbies rather than get straight down to business? Or is he a diligent rottweiler who is all work and no play? Is he a toy breed that needs extra attention and your unwavering focus? Do some digging and find out! First impressions count, and most employers know within minutes, sometimes seconds, if you're the right dog for the job simply by how you present yourself.

All dogs like to perform an unexpected trick now and then, but don't try anything tricky when filling out your resume or providing "ruff"-erences. Remember, one of the primary doggie traits is loyalty. Alpha Dogs want to know that you are loyal and honest and that they can trust you with the keys to their work den. Put your best paw forward! And don't embellish work history or create faux rufferences or your potential employer will find out when they do their own digging into your puppy past! Speaking of digging, employers will Google you, too. What does your Internet trail look like? Is it paw-sitive or negative? Make sure your Internet paw prints will work to your advantage, assuring your prospective new employer that it would be a wise choice to adopt you. And this dog trail goes both ways. If you find out your potential employer is a Cruella De Ville, maybe consider taking your spotted coat somewhere else.

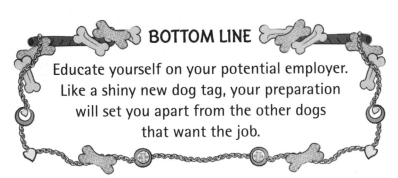

BOTTOM LINE

Educate yourself on your potential employer. Like a shiny new dog tag, your preparation will set you apart from the other dogs that want the job.

Be a Designer Mutt Breed: A Hot Commodity

Designer dogs and your everyday mutt are the result of different breeding that results in a dynamic set of desirable traits. Mutts and designer breeds blend the best of both worlds with attributes of many well-liked breeds. They are multifaceted, which is essential in the business world.

Make yourself a designer mutt by showcasing your hot commodities. Think exotic. Think unique. Think hypoallergenic (okay, maybe not in the business sense). Versatility is key. The more you can fashion yourself after a mutt or designer breed, the more likely you'll be picked up and shown off. In this time of economic difficulty, being a "slasher," or human multi-breed, is essential. Learn from a Brat: part Boston terrier and part rat terrier. A rat terrier is intelligent, active, and rare while a Boston terrier is friendly, strong, and eager to please. So you see why in business, being a Brat pays off? Which sounds more marketable: being a graphic designer or being a graphic and web designer/photographer/editor?

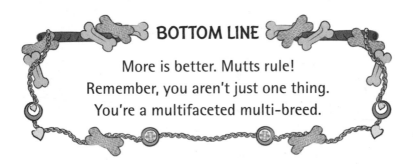

BOTTOM LINE

More is better. Mutts rule!
Remember, you aren't just one thing.
You're a multifaceted multi-breed.

Instinctive Puppy Play

Keep your conversation flowing nicely while interviewing. Think of instinctual puppy play—gentle, fun, not too aggressive, and certainly no big bites. An employer is going to be turned off by too much (or any) growling, overeagerness, or whining—not to mention aggression! Showing just enough personality but not too much is vital. So how do you know if you've gone too far? Check your interviewer's body language—are they playing or fleeing? If you need some pointers on exactly how this animal play works, just go to the dog park. Which dog is getting the most attention, and which dogs are the other canines avoiding? We all know that overly aggressive puppy in the dog park.

BOTTOM LINE

Be the puppy in the park that everyone wants to socialize with.

Shake Like a Dog!

Every well-behaved dog knows how to "shake." It's no surprise that every powerhouse businessperson knows how to shake too. It's important to know handshake etiquette: firm and direct with ample eye contact. Think of your handshake as a toast between hands rather than between glasses. If you squeeze too hard, your champagne flute will break. Since dogs can only demonstrate their behavior and appreciation nonverbally, a good shake means a genuine thank-you. Unless, of course, they are shaking just to get a treat—hey, we've all done it. Just remember that your handshake is meant to be a gracious thank you.

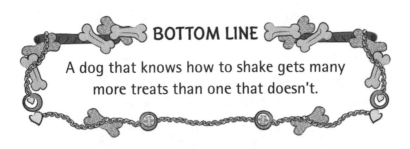

BOTTOM LINE

A dog that knows how to shake gets many more treats than one that doesn't.

2

FIRST DAYS
AT THE DOG PARK

NOW THAT YOU'VE BEEN ADOPTED into a company, it's time to get trained. While you are being trained, much like a puppy or any dog new to a home, you will need to listen and be obedient. You want to show your new parent—no, let me rephrase that—you want to show your new *adopter* that they made a very good choice in adopting you by jumping through the training hoops they put before you.

Dogs are smart. In fact, dogs are so smart that although they may feign being trained, in reality it's the other way around. They're staking their territory and beginning to train their pet parent. Once you've learned this formula, you're well on your way to gaining control and establishing exactly who's the boss—not with words, but with actions. Think about it. How else did Leona Helmsley's dog Trouble train her pet parent to bequeath her a million-dollar fortune? Actions, not words.

Your Boss Will Train You, Too

Before you jump into the trainer's ring and start training everyone who crosses your path, remember that you are the new pup in the office litter and must exercise a bit of puppy patience. You will have to face the facts: it's time to learn the basic rules and get a training foundation. Fortunately, you've already been housebroken, you are a well-mannered pup, and you can crunch numbers. I know what you're thinking—what's left to learn? It may surprise you to learn that your trainer might know what's best for you, including some things you've never considered before. Your boss chose you for a reason—he or she saw potential in you. Prove your potential and listen. Once you show your boss obedience, willingness, flexibility, and, most importantly, loyalty, he or she will put great trust in you. That trust will set the stage for your ability to turn the tables and begin training your boss.

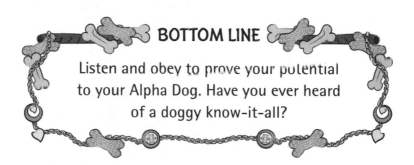

BOTTOM LINE

Listen and obey to prove your potential
to your Alpha Dog. Have you ever heard
of a doggy know-it-all?

Open Doggy Door Policy

Try to create an open-door policy with your boss, co-workers, canine clients, mutt manager, or anyone worth impressing. Be aware of the "chain of command," and don't step on anyone's paws or tail too soon while establishing yourself as one of the leading pups in the pack.

One of the first commands dogs learn in training is "sit." This command works well when going "snout-to-snout" about an important issue. Leave the front door open to your office or create an inviting atmosphere in your doorless cubicle. When your employer or a client walks in to address an important matter, say firmly but in a welcoming manner, "Sit." Maybe throw in a "down" or a "please." They will begin to feel comfortable approaching you with any important issue and vice versa. And look at you, the newbie in the dog park already giving commands that colleagues are following.

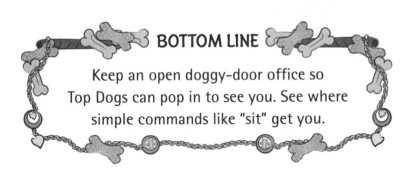

BOTTOM LINE

Keep an open doggy-door office so
Top Dogs can pop in to see you. See where
simple commands like "sit" get you.

Protected Puppy Privacy

As important as it is to have an open-door policy, all dogs originate from wolves that thrived on having their sacred dens all to themselves. Every Top Dog has a private office securely protected by a well-trained guard dog (a secretary, personal assistant or e-mail auto-response) to screen unwanted calls or wild, uninvited scavengers. Make sure to create your own personal space at the office to ensure your greatest productivity, without the other work hounds distracting you with frivolous frolicking and fruitless games of fetch. And make home a place of escape from the pressures of work as well. Since you've carved out this personal space, you have an oasis when the pressures of your work life become a bit too stressful (and everyone knows that work-related stress is sometimes inevitable). Why do you think our dogs hide under the bed?

If you're going to cry, cry in private. And if things get too bad, inform your employer that you plan on taking a vacation or a personal day to retreat to your own home for some much-needed R&R (Retrieving & Releasing). Time away will surely keep you out of the doghouse (where you absolutely DO NOT want to be) and will prevent you from getting into any stress-related dogfights. Not to mention, it will keep your personal life personal— no Top Dog lets it all hang out. They keep it all under the bed.

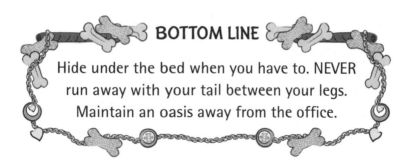

BOTTOM LINE

Hide under the bed when you have to. NEVER run away with your tail between your legs. Maintain an oasis away from the office.

Office-Breaking

We all know the old cliché: "You can't teach an old dog new tricks!" But can you? When your new owner—I mean employer or client—wants you to learn new tricks to improve your work performance, jump enthusiastically into the necessary training program. Who doesn't want to be Best in Show? But remember to retain some control over the situation and teach your Alpha Dog dictator a few new tricks as well. You'll want to be able to mark your territory and leave your scent on the workplace. It's important to begin office-breaking your boss from day one on the job—it will take patience, consistency, and a commitment to reach your ultimate goal! Initiate a friendly, albeit competitive, game of tug-of-war and show your employer that you won't be a pushover. Show that you are capable of supervising and executing some useful, clever ideas of your own. Offer your own special brand of jumping through project hoops to make a lasting impression while claiming your territory. You'll have your employer rolling over to your way of thinking in no time at all.

Remember, everything you accomplish in life is all about delivery. If you underdeliver and do not give 100 percent, people will think of you as lazy and easily forget you. On the other hand, if you go that extra mile and overdeliver, you will gain the respect of the pack as well as the Top Dog.

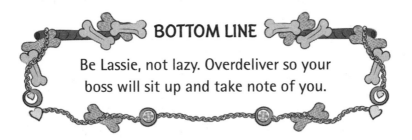

BOTTOM LINE

Be Lassie, not lazy. Overdeliver so your boss will sit up and take note of you.

Working Like a Dog: Overtime Hours

Dogs actually want to work, and they take pride in performing their best at a job for just a pat on the head. If only you could get your employees to do the same. Dogs are willing to put in the hours required if the job suits the breed. Look at the working and herding groups of dogs! It is awe-inspiring to watch a herding dog in action. They work with pride, passion, and grace. As for working overtime, do it. Dogs work with love and pet parents see it. That's why they're never upset after a long day of work and sleep for hours—and hours and hours. But remember, it's up to you to say enough is enough. If you are getting paid and don't mind working late hours, so be it. But if you feel your employer is taking advantage of your good nature and giving you too many projects outside your original job description without pay, then firmly use the command "no." You don't have to say it exactly like that . . . try a gentle variation such as, "I'm not able to stay late after this week, but I appreciate the extra responsibility you've trusted me with." Chances are your boss will respect your moxie and certainly will think twice before asking you to overwork yourself again.

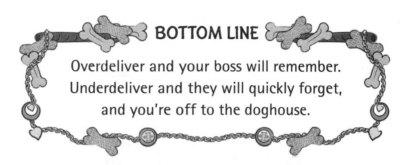

BOTTOM LINE

Overdeliver and your boss will remember. Underdeliver and they will quickly forget, and you're off to the doghouse.

Dogs Understand "No," Not "Yes"!

Because you're new to the puppy park, you want to be accommodating. Of course, you will pick up slack where the other dogs drag behind. Be aware, however, that you cannot say "yes" to everything. If you become the "yes" man or woman that everyone counts on, and you'll have no time to teach your boss to roll over! That's not to say there's never a place for "yes," but as I mentioned before, "no" is sometimes more helpful than "yes." Look at our dogs! They understand "good boy," but not "yes." They adore being accommodating, but sometimes when we need something from them, we get a canine "no"—an inaudible sound that can come in the form of ignoring us, hiding, or heading in the opposite direction. Whatever it is, we know what their "no" looks like. Try emulating it at the office (when appropriate) and see what happens. But whatever you do, don't make excuses. Our dogs don't do that. Your "no" is enough.

BOTTOM LINE

Dogs understand "no."
They don't understand "yes."

PROFESSIONALISM: BE THE WINNING BREED THAT YOU ARE!

NOW THAT YOU'VE BEEN ADOPTED and have started your training, it's time to look and act the part. Pet horror stories happen when pet parents adopt a dog that looks sweet and innocent but ends up being vicious (and hates taking baths). Don't be that dog. Be the best employee you can be by following some simple rules that will help you make a positive impression every day.

Dog Team Player

When the Top Dog or client is looking for a leader of the pack that deserves to be awarded with the big, juicy bone, they will be watching to see who can work and play alongside the other dogs at the office. Even though everyone else will be panting for the prize, harness the lead by demonstrating your leadership qualities whenever you can, even if it's as simple as taking the initiative to organize your company holiday party. You will get noticed as the friendly take-charge canine with Alpha Dog potential. So watch out, canine coworkers!

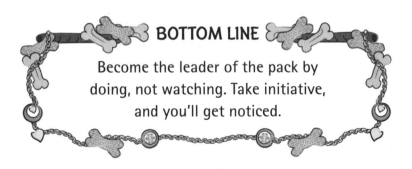

BOTTOM LINE

Become the leader of the pack by doing, not watching. Take initiative, and you'll get noticed.

Animal Magnetism Appearances

Appearances are important, and sometimes they are everything, so do not hide your true animal magnetism behind a sloppy appearance. Make an appointment with your local groomer and *stay* groomed. It may sound silly, but maintaining your nails, hair, facial hair, and personal hygiene are all vital. If you feel like you are the Best in Show, why not emulate that via your appearance. Be confident. Win that ribbon.

In terms of doggy designs, you don't have to break your bank to look good. Pay one visit to your local thrift store (or a few of them, just for fun) and your jaw may drop at the affordable prices and wide variety of styles they offer. Choose an everyday piece like a suit, combine it with a stylish belt or other accessories, and you're on track. You want your employer to see you as a savvy player with both business *and* fashion sense. Think about being up for a promotion. You and your competitor are both completely qualified, but who *looks* better? Who is going to impress clients and dazzle bystanders? The one with the primped pedigree.

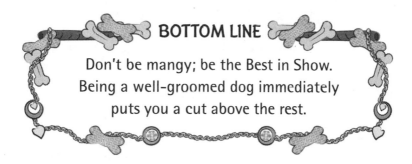

BOTTOM LINE

Don't be mangy; be the Best in Show.
Being a well-groomed dog immediately
puts you a cut above the rest.

Time Is Money—In Dog Years, That's 7x the Value!

If the early bird gets the worm, then the early dog must get the bone! Top Dogs look down on those who have problems arriving on time to the workplace, so it is important to make sure you not only arrive on time but that you arrive a few minutes early, just to be safe. For example, if you are scheduled to start at 9, arrive at 8:50 so you have a few minutes to get settled and ready to start the day. If you arrive late, dragging your tail lazily, or frantically run through the door panting, you are not only being disrespectful, but you are also wasting everyone else's time. Dog years are seven to one, which makes our time a valuable asset that we cannot replace—seven times over! Think of each minute as seven, then try to explain why you are ten minutes late. That's over an hour in dog time!

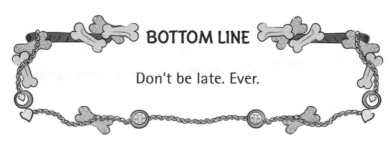

BOTTOM LINE

Don't be late. Ever.

No Panting! Stay Stress-Free

Have you ever seen a stressed-out sheepdog? What about a worried Weimaraner? Even if they do feel stressed, most dogs are good at hiding it (we won't mention high-strung schnauzers). You should do the same. Remaining a non-anxious presence in the workplace is key to earning the trust and confidence of those with the power to move you up in the company. No one wants to hear about stress. Well, maybe a therapist, but you're paying them. It's bad energy. It's a faux-paw.

Stress in the workplace leads to diminished productivity and compromised work relationships. Stress, much like yawning, can also be contagious—and you don't want to be identified as Patient Zero. When faced with stressful situations, try some deep panting, or breathing. Step away from the stressor for a bit, get a clearer head, and see if when you reengage you are able to recognize solutions that weren't apparent before when you were steeped in stress. You will be awarded Best in Show if you can learn to exhibit your incredible ability to remain calm and non-anxious in the middle of stressful work situations.

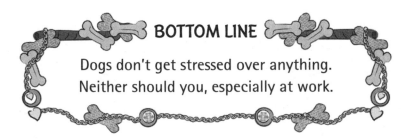

BOTTOM LINE

Dogs don't get stressed over anything.
Neither should you, especially at work.

Petiquette

If you're a pet parent (or any kind of parent for that matter), you've surely had the unfortunate experience of having to explain your pet's (or child's) poor "petiquette." What dog hasn't greeted guests with a friendly nose to the crotch? Embarrassing, right? For them it's the appropriate thing to do, but most guests have a different idea of what's appropriate and acceptable. Keep your eyes and ears alert for workplace norms. How do people greet one another—first name, Mr./Ms., or "Hey, you!"? Is the atmosphere casual or more formal? Always dress and behave accordingly. Does everyone share a lunchroom? While you may think the sardines you bring for lunch every day smell tantalizing, your coworkers may be left gagging from the pungent odor. Make sure your behavior is always considerate, respectful, and appropriate to the office culture. Any questions? Consult Miss Petiquette. This is an easy way to get ahead. Just ask any well-behaved dog. Proper petiquette is the reason the dog accessories market is a billion-dollar industry. Good dogs get rewarded.

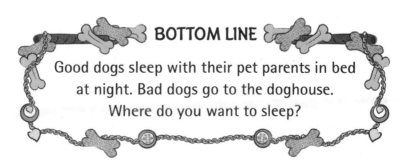

BOTTOM LINE

Good dogs sleep with their pet parents in bed at night. Bad dogs go to the doghouse. Where do you want to sleep?

Personal Life in Check

If your dog were able to speak, he might tell you about his crush on the prissy poodle next door, how much he hates being picked up by crazy Aunt Betsy who smells like bleach, or that he is thinking of running away to find himself. But of course, except for the few brilliant dogs on YouTube that can howl "Rie ruh roo!", canines are pretty close-mouthed about their personal issues. That's how it should be at work. Don't fall victim to letting your personal life get in the way of your work life. Much like stress, a foul mood due to outside circumstances can be contagious, so don't allow difficulties in your personal life to negatively impact your work life. Take a personal day if you must.

BOTTOM LINE

Leave the doggie drama
at the doggy door.

"The average dog is a nicer person than the average person."

—ANDREW A. ROONEY

Dirty Dog Harassment

If a dirty hound dog (fellow employee) gets frisky with you at the office or starts sniffing you in all the wrong places, then it's time yet again to use that firm "no" command. If that same "in heat" dog continues his or her inappropriate manner, it's time to go to the Top Dog and inform them that they have a wild wolf in their midst. Your employer will thank you for preventing future uncomfortable situations and avoiding any legal ramifications that might have ensued. Your pawsy pursuer may respond well to discipline, or he or she may be sent to the pound to think about changing their ways. Either way, you will be able to get back to chasing balls and digging up tasty bones instead of expending your energy trying to duck a dirty dog.

BOTTOM LINE

Uninvited puppy love has no place at work.

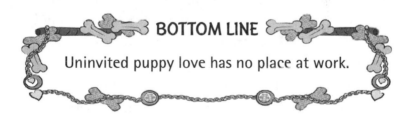

"If you pick up a starving dog and make him prosperous, he will not bite you; that is the principal difference between a dog and a man." —MARK TWAIN

Workplace Eats & Liquid Treats

If given access to a constantly full food bowl, most dogs would eat themselves into obesity. That's why dog owners typically ration out the appropriate amount of food for the day. Same with treats. Even though it's fun to reward Fido with yummy tidbits for good behavior, a wise pet parent knows that too much of a good thing can lead to a bad outcome—literally! Apply this same wisdom to your workplace. Snacking all day at your workspace or in your office can be distracting for the entire staff (think crunchy chips and crispy crackers), and it may leave the impression with your employer that your focus is more on filling your belly than on fulfilling your corporate duties. Plus, it can lead to a paunchy pooch. So minimize your snacking, and save your appetite for your designated lunch period. You are what you eat, you know. You don't want that Alpha Dog thinking you're Oreos and Twizzlers.

Speaking of lunch, if you go out to eat, resist the urge to wash everything down with a liquid treat that could leave you tipsy. This also applies to lunch meetings and holiday or corporate parties you might attend—drunk dogs can make messes that are embarrassing and tough to clean up! And if you see that your boss's bowl is always full, pull him or her aside and use a distraction technique to help prevent an awkward faux paw.

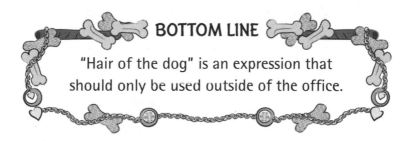

BOTTOM LINE

"Hair of the dog" is an expression that should only be used outside of the office.

Let Sleeping Dogs Lie!

Dogs sleep a lot. So when they're ready to chase that Frisbee or win that game of tug-of-war, they are up to the challenge. Whether you are a natural night owl, an early bird that hops up before the crack of dawn, or an insomniac who finds it hard to sleep at all, getting enough sleep is a key to success. Careless mistakes are made when we're running on too little sleep, so if you're not sleeping well, talk to your doctor about it. Find out what's pre-

venting you from getting enough zzzzs—sleep is a necessity, *not* a luxury. When the alarm goes off, it means wake up, get to work, and do the best possible job you can. You can't just let "sleeping dogs lie." With sufficient sleep on a regular basis, you will be able to hop up on the right side of the dog bed every day. Your health, energy, and focus will be on point, readying you for the dog park where you will finally be able to teach your boss to roll over.

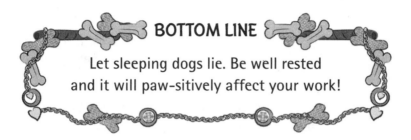

BOTTOM LINE

Let sleeping dogs lie. Be well rested
and it will paw-sitively affect your work!

"What counts is not necessarily
the size of the dog in the fight;
it's the size of the fight in the dog."

—DWIGHT D. EISENHOWER

4

BECOMING THE MASTER

S O YOU'VE BEEN WORKING AT YOUR PLACE of employment for some time now, or your business has finally gotten off the ground, and you've laid the groundwork to finally teach your boss or your top client to roll over. You look the part, you've done everything you can personally to succeed, you've proven yourself, and you've put out the feelers. You've spent considerable time studying your Alpha Dog—getting to know his or her likes, dislikes, and how you can best grab their attention. So let the real training begin.

Time to Play "Name That Name"!

Whether he is Mr. Bojangles, Mrs. Robinson, or simply *Carl,* names are very important in the business world. When we train our dogs, we constantly use their names. "Come here, Rex." "Chopper, SIT!" "Lucky . . . no!" Name play is essential in training techniques. Who doesn't love to hear the sound of their own name? Subconsciously your boss will hear your call as a respectful command.

Use the name in its most appropriate form—by now you know exactly how your Alpha Dog wants to be addressed. "Pete, I have those files for you," sounds a lot different than, "Here are those files." This is increasingly important when making requests or personal statements as well as when giving responses. When you need to respond in the negative to a request, "Mrs. Jones, I cannot stay late," is direct and to the point while still giving her the pleasure of hearing her name out loud. Play with intonation, placement of the name within the statement, and body language. You will be surprised at how a name attached to a spoken command with the proper tone can produce amazing results. Any pet parent can attest—dogs come when you call them by name.

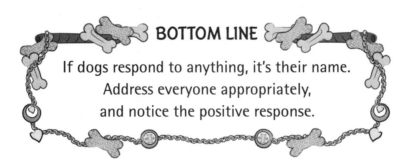

BOTTOM LINE

If dogs respond to anything, it's their name.
Address everyone appropriately,
and notice the positive response.

"Outside of a dog, a book is man's best friend.
Inside of a dog, it's too dark to read."

—GROUCHO MARX

Lap Dog Loyalty

Who is really in control, the person with a dog on their lap or the dog that is SITTING on the lap? The truth is, the lap dog has their pet parent "whipped." But it didn't start out that way. The lap dog demonstrated loyalty to earn the place of honor there on its parent's lap. So maybe you have to be the lap dog to your Alpha Dog for a while. Once the loyalty is built, your Alpha Dog won't know what to do without you. You will be the person your boss turns to in moments of crisis. You're the one with the big ideas. You're the one who's been there. You're the one first in line for a promotion. Being a lap dog can be a joy, but beware of jealousy. You're bound to come across some other dogs, probably lap dog wannabes, who'd love to knock you off that lap and take your place.

BOTTOM LINE

Lap dogs bask in luxury.

Top Dog Treats

Dogs love their treats and will do just about anything you ask to earn a bite of their favorite snack! But few dogs do tricks without a treat. Remember that your employer is the Top Dog, and he loves treats too. If you've had your eye on that corner office, promotion, pay raise, or bonus, then apply the treat theory to your employer.

Yes, you will have to be more clever and calculating with your employer than with Bingo when applying the treat theory. But it will work if you do your research. We all like to get treats, and the Top Dog is no different. So what makes your Top Dog's tail wag? Does he or she like football game tickets, good seats at the symphony, great dining, sci-fi books, Swiss chocolates, or rowdy rock concerts? You get the idea. Cook them their favorite cupcakes! Don't hesitate to provide your employer with their favorite treat to leave a lasting impression.

If your fellow coworkers accuse you of sniffing your boss's butt, ignore them. It will be you that your employer remembers when it's time to fill that corner office or sign those bonus checks. Woof woof all the way to the bank!

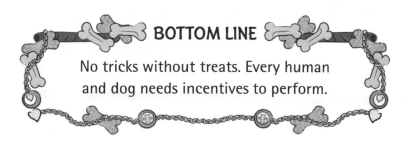

BOTTOM LINE

No tricks without treats. Every human and dog needs incentives to perform.

Barking Boss

If your employer tends to bark loudly at you in the presence of fellow employees, it's up to you to take control and use the "no" command. Maybe his or her yelping is due to work-related or personal anxiety or insecurity. Try to be understanding and maintain a cool, calm attitude. At the same time, it's up to you to train your boss that mistreating you in this way is unacceptable. Repeat the "no" command firmly but respectfully until your Alpha Dog backs away and stops barking at you. She might even slink away with her tail between her legs as she considers her inappropriate actions. You've helped your boss learn a valuable lesson.

If your barking boss has reason to yap, avoid using "no" altogether. Accept responsibility for your actions. Hey, maybe even try giving them the puppy eyes. It's up to you to take ownership and remedy the situation as best you can. The sooner you do it, the more respect you will garner.

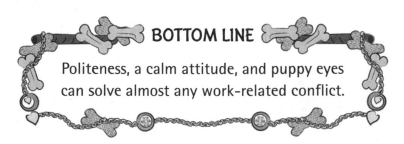

BOTTOM LINE

Politeness, a calm attitude, and puppy eyes can solve almost any work-related conflict.

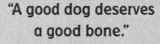

"A good dog deserves
a good bone."
—US PROVERB

The Business Leash

Doggy decorum and discipline are necessary in order to maintain a productive workplace atmosphere. Here's where the leash comes into play. Some employers let their employees run on a long leash and give them lots of freedom, while others like to keep a short leash. It's your job to figure out which approach your employer uses and then, in turn, to cooperate. Don't be the dog that constantly pulls at the leash, frustrating and exhausting its owner. Be the dog that leaves some slack in the leash, no matter how much or how little space your employer gives you to sniff around. When your employer trusts you to behave, you will find yourself with a longer leash and more freedom.

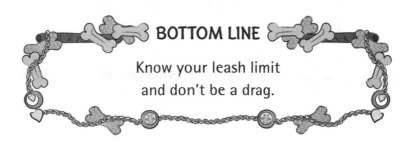

BOTTOM LINE

Know your leash limit
and don't be a drag.

Superior Game of Stare

One workplace trick the Alpha Dog knows and has probably mastered is the stare. The stare is the premiere body language tool for dominating the workplace, a meeting, negotiations, jealous fellow employees, your boss, or a potential client. Here's the trick: when first making eye contact with someone that you are doing business with or that you want to control professionally, don't blink or look away first! All Alpha Dogs are keenly aware that the first person to lose the game of stare loses the right to dominate the coveted territory. I suggest you practice staring at yourself in the mirror, battle it out with a trusted friend (and try not to howl with laughter like when you were kids), or go blink-to-blink with your own canine counterpart.

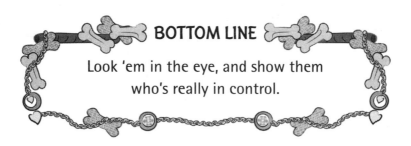

BOTTOM LINE

Look 'em in the eye, and show them who's really in control.

"The biggest dog has been a pup."

—JOAQUIN MILLER, US POET

Show No Fear

When an animal feels fear, predators often seize the opportunity to attack. In business, fear is toxic. For entrepreneurs, doubting yourself or having unresolved personal fears can implode your business. If you ever want to be your own Top Dog or gain the respect of the Alpha Dog at work, you have to be fearless. How do you do this? Resolve for yourself that the worst thing you have to fear is looking back and realizing you were too afraid to go for it. And then go for it. Be that German shepherd, feisty terrier, or dominating Doberman that doesn't back down from anything. You'll be astounded by the respect you get when you saunter down the office hallways.

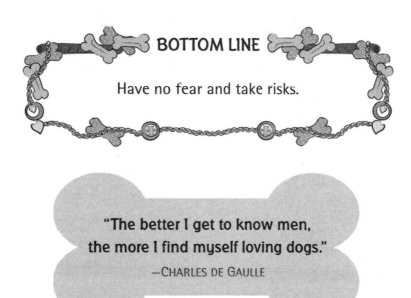

BOTTOM LINE

Have no fear and take risks.

"The better I get to know men, the more I find myself loving dogs."

—CHARLES DE GAULLE

Don't Wind Up in the Doghouse

Some call it time-out. Children know it as getting sent to the corner. The 60-and-over crowd used dunce caps. But many of us grown-ups know it as the doghouse, and none of us want to be there. The doghouse is on the outside, and your goal is to get on the inside. When you're in the doghouse, you're expected to keep quiet and put your head down. Your number-one tip in business may be to stay out of the doghouse.

BOTTOM LINE

It's cold outside in the doghouse.
Don't end up there because of bad behavior.

FINALLY

Regal Resigning

WHEN THE TIME HAS COME FOR YOU to stray and venture out to greener professional pastures because you feel your career is going to the dogs, make nice with your current employer and give proper notice. Top Dogs usually run in the same circles, and you'll want to train the employer you're leaving to give you a good reference in the future.

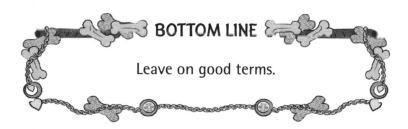

BOTTOM LINE

Leave on good terms.

Man's Best Friend

Even though your boss may look like a big, mean, vicious attack dog, he or she is really there to help you. They may show their teeth sometimes, but they only want you to succeed and, in turn, to help the company succeed as well. Isn't that why they hired you? Do not be afraid to ask for guidance from the Alpha Dog. As intimidating as they may look, the "big dog on campus" would love to give you advice and help you out.

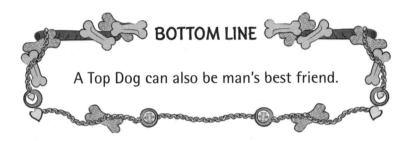

BOTTOM LINE

A Top Dog can also be man's best friend.

Be Paw-sitive

When you waltz through life with a positive attitude and a wagging tail, the sky looks bluer and the flowers smell sweeter! Have you ever noticed how excited dogs get when people enter a shelter? They jump up and wag their tails even though they may be frightened and lonely. Dogs get adopted because they have a positive attitude. And positive reinforcement is the best kind of training there is because it gives you something worthwhile to work for instead of just scaring you into performing better.

Positivity also involves forgiving and moving on. For example, if your dog has an accident in the house, you teach him that this isn't the appropriate place to go potty. Then you forget about it and move forward. It is important to get over things and not get stuck in the past. If your team loses a game, you put that in the past and simply win the next one. If your girlfriend or boyfriend dumps you, you go out and meet someone better. A real "leader of the pack" understands that we all make mistakes, and that fussing over them will not only slow down work, but it will also prevent us from learning from these mistakes. As Elvis Costello once sang, "Accidents will happen." When you feel you've been wronged in the workplace, it's important to forgive, forget, and move on.

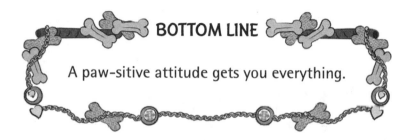

BOTTOM LINE

A paw-sitive attitude gets you everything.

Roll Over!

When a dog rolls over, it means they are scratching their back, stretching, or obeying a playful command. Basically, they are having fun. Having a full-time job does not always have to be about "working like a dog." Find ways to make your work environment fun. Organize a regular potluck lunch for office birthdays or suggest a themed dress day once a month. Keep it within the professional boundaries though. The Alpha Dog should not have to send you to obedience school for you to learn how to behave in a work environment.

BOTTOM LINE

Working like a dog isn't bad
when you enjoy your work.

"Any man who does not like dogs
and want them about, does not
deserve to be in the White House."

—CALVIN COOLIDGE

Who Runs in Your Top Dog's Pack?

Dogs like to run in packs, and so do CEOs, CFOs, business owners, founders, executives, and managers. You can learn a lot about your boss, and how to get him or her to roll over, by observing the company they keep. You can see Alpha Dogs running around together at restaurants, golf courses, sporting events, and social gatherings—any place where they can mark their territory.

While studying your boss's friends and colleagues for training tips, don't overlook your boss's furry friend. People usually pick a canine breed by identifying with certain attributes that the dog possesses; they instantly connect! By knowing more about the type of dog your boss chose as a companion, you can easily read how to train them and thereby get what you've been digging for, like that Alpha Dog promotion or more treats in your paycheck!

There are over 175 breeds of dogs, and every dog breed belongs to a group. The seven primary groups recognized by the American Kennel Club are Sporting, Hound, Working, Terrier, Toy, Non-Sporting, and Herding. Of course, there's another group we all know and love, my personal favorite—Mutts! No matter the breed or group, the luckiest of ALL dogs are those we call Adopted. Whether pure bred, designer, or mutt, these dogs just appreciate being given a chance to prove their undying devotion and love.

The Spunky Sporting

Dogs in the spirited sporting group live for the proverbial hunt. Lovable and high-octane breeds that belong to this active crowd are pointers, retrievers, setters, and spaniels. If your boss has a pooch associated with this pack, you'd better take your daily vitamins to keep up! The sporty boss is driven, naturally alert, and always on the go— looking for the next big treat.

The key to training this corporate power player who jumps through hoops to get from one meeting to the next is control! By proving you can take over the reins and help lighten your sporty CEO's load, you'll train your boss to make you an integral part of the winning team. If you are an irreplaceable asset in the business dog run, guess what? You're marking your territory, and you *will* be noticed!

True to their name, the sporty Alpha Dog needs lots (and I do mean lots) of exercise and an outlet for their inner wolf. Buddy up and suggest a joint run in the local dog park before or after work or a free pass to your gym.

Media queen Oprah Winfrey has two cocker spaniels that she parents while also spearheading Oprah Winfrey Network. High energy? That's an understatement.

SPORTING DOG PROFESSIONS: Entrepreneur, architect, interior designer, restaurant and pub owner (especially near water), entertainer, athlete, medical professional, law enforcement official.

The Howling Hound

A Top Dog knows that sniffing out a hot lead and following its trail is the key to success. The hound group is born with a keen sense for scents; they have a real nose for business and can smell a deal from a mile away! Pharaoh hounds, beagles, Norwegian elkhounds, and Afghans are a part of this unique pooch party.

If your head honcho is the pet parent to a clever canine from this group, you can expect a lot of strategizing during long nights at the office! The hound has incredible stamina and doesn't mind working like a dog, and it actually expects the same from you. This is where a bone of contention might lie between the two of you. If you've been working late nights and your family forgets what your mug looks like, it might be time to let the hound at the helm know it's time to lighten up a bit.

But beware: the hound breeds are known for having a loud baying bark and aren't afraid to yap back. Instead of a "no" command, offer to take your leader of the pack for a treat, like lunch or dinner, and be a doggy diplomat in your delivery. Suggest that you don't mind working long days on occasion but that you do have pups of your own at home and they're starting to feel like strays. This approach should keep you out of the doghouse.

Founder of Virgin Media, explorer, and inventor Richard Branson and his bloodhound named Sushi have proven to be a highly successful team.

HOUND DOG PROFESSIONS: Educator, stock broker, social media guru, international trade expert, farmer, oil and natural gas exploration worker.

The Working Warriors

Heave-ho! The working canines are the CEOs that don't mind getting their paws dirty. This group of team players consists of Dobermans, schnauzers, Siberian huskies, Great Danes, and boxers. If your workplace Alpha Dog identifies with this breed group, you can expect a strong and protective boss who's willing to listen to new tricks that you've come up with to improve business. The working warriors wag their tails when someone on their team earnestly shares innovative, productive techniques.

What the working warrior Top Dog wants most is financial and territorial security. If this is threatened in any way, he or she will instantly react and defend at all costs! Expect a dog fight to the bitter end if they think anyone on their team has been disloyal or is selling company secrets. Keep your paws clean and run for the hills if anyone in your office tries to get your leash tangled up where there's company dirt or foul play. It will be difficult to retrain your working boss to trust you again, especially if they feel you haven't appreciated the opportunity they have given you in the company. It's the "once bitten, twice shy" scenario with them all the way. Stay on track, praise your working boss, and reap the benefits.

Legendary Apple founder, working warrior, and visionary creator Steve Jobs was a proud pet parent to a husky named Beau!

WORKING DOG PROFESSIONS: Military personnel, spy, investigative news reporter, legal analyst or lawyer, inventor, engineer, construction worker, real estate developer, private investigator.

The Tough Terriers

Don't mess with the terrier tribe! The terriers have a killer instinct. They will hunt down and get rid of any competition that gets in the way of their success! Canines that belong to this group include the bull terrier, cairn terrier, Jack Russell terrier, and West Highland white terrier. If this is your boss's canine by choice, you may have met your career match.

Whatever you do, don't argue and act like a "know-it-all" with your terrier boss! They simply won't roll over, and will continue the argument until they've made their point and you walk out of their office with your tail between your legs. Yes, this troupe is tough! It's going to take constant determination and patience on your part to win over the terrier. *But,* once you have proven yourself and the terrier considers you one of his or her own, you're in!

The feisty and energized Top Dog terrier likes and expects instant positive results. If you over-deliver and bring home the bacon bits, you'll have them eating out of the palm of your hand. And you'll certainly enjoy being the company lap dog!

Pet Airlines founders Dan Wiesel and Alysa Binder were inspired to start the pet-friendly airlines by their terrier, Zoe, after experiencing difficulty traveling with their little pup. Fashion designer Diane von Furstenberg, media mogul Rupert Murdoch, and Secretary of State Hillary Clinton all belong to the exclusive terrier group.

TERRIER DOG PROFESSIONS: Business consultant, investment banker, mediator, entertainment producer, entrepreneur, promoter, advertising executive, public relations specialist, politician.

The Trainable Toys

Good things come in small packages! The toy group might be diminutive in stature, but they're intelligent and are fighters down to their furry core. This band of breeds includes the Maltese, Chinese crested, poodle, shih tzu, Pomeranian, Chihuahua, and Havanese. The toys should not be toyed with. If your boss is so self-assured and secure that he or she picked a toy breed from this group, expect some pleasant surprises.

The toy boss probably prefers having their office in the big city, and they don't mind smaller dwelling spaces. Toy Top Dogs can really change character with their busi-

ness approach—one minute charming and zen, the next minute mischievous. You're going to have to stay on your toes with this CFO chameleon.

But here's the trick: the toy Top Dog can be trained once you know what makes them tick! If you can find out what your toy boss wishes to achieve in the global market, and you help make this happen on a consistent day-to-day basis, you have found the key to *your* success. This will mean dispensing a marginal daily treat for your toy chief, and with each single treat, you will move a little closer to the "roll over" command. Tricky business, yes! But isn't all business?

The inspiration for *Animal Fair Media,* pet icon, and charismatic Maltese, our beloved Lucky Diamond is in the toy group. Lucky is the toy that helped save countless animal lives and brought national awareness to animal rescue!

TOY DOG PROFESSIONS: Entertainer, therapist, performer, party and event planner, scientific researcher, clothing designer, corporate CEO.

The Not So Sporting

The non-sporting group is the potpourri of pups—you never know what kind of executive you're going to get! *Diversity* is the key word here. Non-sporting Top Dogs can have different personalities, come in variable sizes, wear unique clothing, and vary greatly in appearance. Some breeds associated with this eclectic crowd are the French poodle, Lhasa apso, Chinese Shar-Pei, and bichon frise.

If the person you professionally answer to has a breed from this bunch, you're going to have to be on your toes (improvisational acting classes might help). Take some time studying your Alpha Dog subject and get a feel for what type of training might be the most productive. There just isn't a set code for these CEOs. Your boss might one day walk in the office sporting a tailored suit (corporate mode) and the next day wearing jeans and a button down (casual mode). Obviously, when your chief of staff is dressed down, it will be easier to get them to roll over with simple requests like "sit" and "stay." On the other paw, when your boss is in a more corporate "modus operandi," back off and let him or her know *you* are the one who's doing the listening.

Again, being spontaneous and going with the flow will be a winning attribute when pleasing the non-sporting group. Whatever you do, don't buy these leaders tickets to a sporting event as a way to impress—remember, they are non-sporting! A dinner at a Thai or Indian restaurant, tickets to the opera or foreign film, a book about the Seven Wonders of the World—all are gifts that will elicit the positive response you're barking for!

New York City mayor and Bloomberg Media head honcho Michael Bloomberg is a poodle boss; *America's Got Talent* and radio talk show host Howard Stern is a bulldog bigwig; and home and garden entrepreneur Martha Stewart is the proud owner of a chow chow.

NON-SPORTING DOG PROFESSIONS: Clothings designer, scientist, publisher, inventor, performer, film director, musician, travel agent.

The Happy Herders

Where's the networking party? The happy herders are the Alpha Dogs that enjoy being a part of the winners circle, something bigger than just themselves. The herders want to rally people together, including their underlings, with an eye on the prize. Herders have a special business instinct for controlling the movement of others while still encouraging the team. If your herder head walks a border collie, German shepherd, puli, Bouvier des Flandres, or Welsh corgi on the weekends, you are dealing with an intelligent boss.

Your herder honcho wants a team player that can really go after competitors, with the hopes of eventually acquiring and absorbing the rogue company. You can train your boss to recognize your talents by finding out where the competition's Achilles' heel lies, then offering a strategic plan to nip at it. This CEO group is actually fun and friendly, somewhat easy to train, and always open to suggestions.

Since the herder executive wants to lead the way and be among crowds of savvy business types, sniff out all the latest industry-related expos, social media conferences, and exciting events across the country. Prepare a slick presentation detailing why your company simply must be a part of these happenings, and nine times out of ten, your herder boss will say bow WOW! And you've earned points for having an eye out for the business. Want to score double dog points? Find a huge outdoor event where the herder boss can meet and run with other Top

Dogs! Their desire is to be in a pack with other influential dogs. Prove you belong in that group as well.

Facebook founder and social media mogul Mark Zuckerberg's puli named Beast has his own Facebook page . . . and has been "Liked"!

HERDER DOG PROFESSIONS: Athlete, social media mogul, transportation specialist, fashion consultant, telecommunications director, architect, educator, hotel and resort personnel, gallery owner, automotive mechanic.

The Mysterious Mutt

This group isn't recognized by the American Kennel Club, but those of us who love a mutt know that they are the most loyal, loving canines you will ever find. But here's the thing—you're never quite sure what you're going to get from a mutt manager! This business group can be a mix of all the above groups, and if your boss has a mutt as a sidekick, let the business games begin! For example: Your boss's canine companion is a "border beagle"— that's part beagle (howling hound) and part border collie (herder). Imagine a company conference meeting where your mutt boss herds everyone in the office together and barks the entire time with no one getting a word in edgewise. Or maybe your mutt Top Dog is part schnauzer (working) and part cocker spaniel (sporting). If you can make the workplace both fun and productive, you will be this Top Dog's top employee.

Half the fun of having a mutt manager is learning

spontaneity with your training process. One minute you'll catch yourself asking them to "stay" a little longer at the meeting to close the deal and the next initiating a healthy game of fetch when bantering about new business policy. The mysterious mutt mogul can be a canine enigma, but once you figure out how to get this Top Dog to roll over, the treats are all yours!

Dave Duffield is a recognized pioneer in enterprise software and human resources technology and the founder of several companies including Workday and PeopleSoft. He also started Maddie's Fund to help and aid animals in shelters nationwide.

MUTT DOG PROFESSIONS: International trade consultant, media or public relations consultant, entertainer, sports personality, restaurant owner, real estate developer, comedian.

The Adorable Adopter

This isn't a group of dogs. It's a type of Alpha Dog that you *want* as your boss. They are good hearted and the type of Top Dog you want to learn from and have in your life. Anytime you find a boss that chooses to adopt a dog, you've found a gem of a person. This group cares about the underdog and will go the extra mile to make sure their employees are well taken care of and provided for. The fact that this busy CEO took the time out of their busy schedule to go to a shelter and adopt (or foster) simply means that they might adopt you as well and consider you an extended member of their corporate family.

The adopter Alpha Dog is the type of boss that will make sure you have health care and creature comforts in the office. Here's the catch-22—help your adopter Alpha Dog recognize when his or her extreme generosity is becoming a business liability. Train your boss to see that in order to grow the company, you have to discern when to keep and when to give away. You can help your adorable adopter know when it's the right time to adopt more productive pups and extend the office environment with fresh mugs!

Get involved. Suggest to your adopter boss that it would be advantageous for your company to actively participate in community service, outreach programs, and philanthropic organizations that organize events helping people and animals in need. Your boss will jump up and roll over at the idea. Not only will it play to their humanitarian side, but your company will also be viewed (rightfully so) as a group that cares and gives back to the community! This is certainly a win-win.

Ron Conway, a Silicon Valley startup angel investor, along with his rescue dog Coco, funds underdog businesses looking to succeed in the dog-cat-dog world.

ADOPTER DOG PROFESSIONS: Green activist, healthcare worker, United Nations diplomat, farmer, politician, government official, union organizer, childcare worker, entertainer, educator.

Top Dog Pure Bred Group

The following is a list of pure bred dogs. See if you can match your boss to the breed.

Sporting Breeds

Brittany spaniel, pointer, golden retriever, Labrador retriever, Nova Scotia duck tolling retriever, English setter, Gordon setter, Irish setter, Irish red & white setter, American water spaniel, Boykin setter, lumber setter, black cocker spaniel, English cocker spaniel, English springer spaniel, field spaniel, Irish water spaniel, Sussex spaniel, spinone Italiano, vizsla, Weimaraner, wirehaired pointing griffon

Hound Breeds

Afghan hound, American foxhound, American English foxhound, basenji, basset hound, beagle, black & tan coonhound, bloodhound, bluetick coonhound, borzoi, dachshund (short, long, and wire-haired), English foxhound, greyhound, harrier, Ibizan hound, Irish wolfhound, Norwegian elkhound, otterhound, petit basset griffon vendeen, Pharaoh hound, Plott hound, redbone coonhound, Rhodesian ridgeback, saluki, Scottish deerhound, whippet

Working Breeds

Akita, Alaskan malamute, Anatolian shepherd dog, Bernese mountain dog, black Russian terrier, boxer, bullmastiff, Cane Corso, Doberman pinscher, giant schnauzer, great Dane, great Pyrenees, greater Swiss mountain dog, komonder, kuvasz, Leonberger, mastiff, neapolitan mastiff, Portuguese water dog, rottweiler, St. Bernard, Samoyed, Siberian husky, standard schnauzer, Tibetan mastiff

Terrier Breeds

Airedale terrier, American Staffordshire terrier, Australian terrier, Bedlington terrier, border terrier, bull terrier (colored & white), cairn terrier, Cesky terrier, dandie Dinmont terrier, fox terrier (smooth & wire-haired), Glen of Imaal terrier, Irish terrier, Kerry blue terrier, Lakeland terrier, Manchester terrier, miniature terrier (standard), miniature schnauzer, Norfolk terrier, Parson Russell terrier, Scottish terrier, Sealyham terrier, Skye terrier, soft Wheaten terrier, Staffordshire bull terrier, Welsh terrier, West Highland white terrier

Toy Breeds

Affenpincher, Brussels griffon, cavalier King Charles spaniel, Chihuahua (long & smooth coat), Chinese crested, English toy spaniel (King Charles & ruby), Havanese, Italian greyhound, Japanese chin, Maltese, Manchester terrier (toy), miniature pinscher, papillon, Pekingese, Pomeranian, poodle (toy), pug, shih tzu, silky terrier, toy fox terrier, Yorkshire terrier

Non-Sporting Breeds

American Eskimo dog, bichon frise, Boston terrier, bulldog, Chinese Shar-Pei, chow chow, Dalmatian, Finnish spitz, French bulldog, keeshond, Lhasa apso, lowchen, Norwegian lundehund, poodle (miniature & standard), schipperke, Shiba Inu, Tibetan spaniel, Tibetan terrier, Xoloitzcuintli (Mexican hairless)

Herding Breeds

Australian cattle dog, Australian shepherd, bearded collie, beauceron, Belgian malinois, Belgian sheepdog, Belgian tervuren, border collie, Bouvier des Flandres, briard, Canaan dog, Cardigan Welsh corgi, collie (rough & smooth), Entlebucher mountain dog, Finnish lapphund, German shepherd, Norwegian buhund, Icelandic sheepdog, Old English sheepdog, Pembroke Welsh corgi, Polish lowland sheepdog, puli, Pyrenean shepherd, Shetland sheepdog, Swedish vallhund

Mutt

Any combination of the above breed groups!

LOOKING FOR A DOG TO LOVE?

According to the ASPCA (American Society for the Prevention of Cruelty to Animals) approximately 5 million to 7 million companion animals enter animal shelters nationwide every year, and approximately 3 million to 4 million are euthanized (60 percent of dogs and 70 percent of cats). Please visit your local shelter and rescue a dog in need of a loving home. Or find a dog rescue organization that needs people to serve as short-term foster families for dogs until they find their forever home.

ABOUT THE AUTHOR

Wendy Diamond is a social entrepreneur, humanitarian, endangered animal and rescue advocate, the world's premiere pet lifestyle expert, best-selling author, and TV personality. Wendy was born in Chagrin Falls, Ohio, studied at Pine Manor College in Boston, and now resides in New York City with her children, Baby Hope and Pasha. As the tireless voice of disenfranchised animals, Wendy Diamond looks to improve the quality of lives for all animals— homeless, sheltered, endangered, or otherwise.